# Leadership Perspectives

## From the Desk of David Barrett

Volume 1
A Curated Selection of Blog Posts Published

KEBS Publishing, Port Credit, Ontario

# Leadership Perspectives
## From the Desk of David Barrett

Editors: Karen Barrett & Kelly Jones
Typesetting: Me
Cover Design: S2Design

Published by:
KEBS Publishing
1079 Red Pine Crescent
Mississauga ON L5H 4E4

Production © 2015 by KEBS Publishing

ISBN: **1519118392**
ISBN-13: **978-1519118394**

# CONTENTS

# DEDICATION

I dedicate this one Brian – always a support, a critic, an advisor and best of all, a great friend.

# INTRODUCTION

In 2001, I was in the middle of my career as a conference producer. I had founded a series of events for project managers and leaders back in 1997 and by 2001 we were running as many as 15 events around the world a year – now for project managers, leaders and business analysts.

I was standing at the back of the keynote speaker session at ProjectWorld Toronto, 2001 when my friend Derek Sweeney, now running The Sweeney Agency Speaker Bureau, turned to me and said "You see that keynote speaker up there on stage, the one you are paying me $15,000 for? That could easily be you some day."

And thus started my 13 year journey from Conference Director to professional speaker. The road included a lot of preparation, practice, book writing and even the sale of my business to make it happen. But it 2014 it happened.

Now. I was still holding down my 20 year relationship with the Schulich Executive Education Centre, Schulich School of Business, York University in Toronto as the National Program Director for The Centres of Excellence in Project Management and Business Analysis. But this new 'career' would fit very nicely with the new me.

Making the move to a professional speaker involved a lot of advice from a lot of people: write a book or two before you launch; offer to speak to any group for nothing for a while to hone your skills; be ready to accept that not everyone will like you and what you say; and start blogging.

Start Blogging!! I had post a few blogs here and there in the past – but I doubt anyone ever read them. But now I was being told that I needed to produce the written word on a regular basis to attract a following of readers and thus, potentially, future customers.

So I did. January, 2014, I started writing 400-600 words each week and publishing precisely at 2pm EST every Wednesday. I thought I had better put a stake in the ground and make a firm commitment to myself and to potential regular readers.

Believe me when I say that this did not come naturally. I really struggled at first, with the creative process, the weekly commitment and subject matter.

But it worked. I am proud to say that I have never missed one week in the almost two years I have been blogging. My readership isn't huge compared to some (about 700 or so of my 2000 subscribers will read the weekly post) but it does get read.

The best part is that I now hear from people across North America and beyond who actually count on it every Wednesday. Imagine that.

Which brings me to this book. I have already published 3 books: The Power of the Plan, The Keys to Our Success and the Business Analyst's Book of Mentors. I have one more in production: From Strategy to Execution: Bridging the Gap. But I am l always open to new ideas and the latest idea came to me from a close personal friend. He observed that after almost 100 posts there had to be some stuff good enough to publish in a new book.

And here was! The following pages contains my top 30 read blog posts as of September, 2015.

Topics range from pure project management to business analysis. Lots of stuff on leadership: personal and professional and a little on my new space: strategy execution.

Before I send you off, I want to thank my two editors. My primary editor is my wife and partner, Karen. She is the one that prevented my readers from seeing some of the initial garbage that comes from my keyboard. Without her, there is no book, no blog posts, no professional speaking and no fun. Thanks as well to Kelly Jones who was able to pull this all together and tidy it up for you, the reader.

Happy reading and please do not hesitate to feedback, comment or rant at me as you read. Email me at dbarrett@solutionsnetwork.com. And if you have not subscribed yet, join me at www.DavidBarrett.ca.

David

# LEADERSHIP

# THE INSPIRATIONAL LEADER

I have been working through an article from Forbes.com (Top 10 Qualities That Make A Great Leader, Dec. 19, 2012) that listed the top 10 qualities that make a great leader. The last on the list is the "ability to inspire."

I get a lot of calls from people looking at the role of the project manager as a potential career. With no business experience, many are fooled into thinking that a career in project management is achievable.

I will always tell a young person that the key to project management is the role as a leader and the act of inspiring a team to success. Unfortunately, this is very difficult unless you have business experience and subject-matter expertise. You can't lead and inspire without having been there before and appreciating what everyone is going through.

The ability to lead and inspire through your leadership is the key to great leadership success.

So what are we inspiring people to do?

Forbes offers up:

1. "Inspiring your team to see the vision of the successes to come." This is tied to so many other qualities a great leader needs, like: enthusiasm, vision, commitment, confidence. We want to use our personality and expertise to inspire others to see "the vision." When they buy in, we get things done as a team. We are inspired together.

2. "Make your team feel invested in the accomplishments of the company." This tells us to inspire our team by looking back at our accomplishments as opposed to looking forward to the vision. Although we are already so busy and buried in the present, inspiration can very well come from the past.

3. "Being able to inspire your team is great for focusing on the future goals, but it is also important for the current issues." And here we are brought back from the future and then the past to the present. As I have written many times in my blog, plans don't always go as expected. Sometimes the plan goes astray and we need to regroup. Inspiration to our team is vital in times of change and stress.

How do we inspire? Susan M. Heathfield wrote an article entitled "Leadership Inspiration: 10 Leadership Success Secrets" for About.com where she captures the action item clearly. "Passion, purpose, listening and meaning help make a leader inspirational. The ability to communicate that passion, purpose and meaning to others helps establish the inspirational culture of your organization."

Well said. Passion, purpose, listening and meaning.

I challenge all of the leaders out there to list these four words and describe each in terms of their professional lives. What is your passion? Why are you all in this together, or what is your purpose? Are you listening? And where is the meaning to your work?

Answer these clearly and you can be the inspirational leader we are all hoping to work for.

*Originally published August 20, 2014*

# PEOPLE SKILLS OR RESULTS?

Sorry, you can't have both! So says Matthew Lieberman in the *Harvard Business Review* Blog Network http://goo.gl/D2SSsk.

Lieberman suggests that a great leader typically cannot be both a people person and a results-focused leader – they just don't work together. Our brains do not allow for this.

In this article, Lieberman quotes a study from 2009 where 60,000 employees were asked about the characteristics of their leaders. The results:

- The leaders seen as being only strong on results were much less likely to be seen as great leaders overall.
- Those leaders strong only on social skills were less likely to be seen as great leaders as well.
- For the very small portion that were viewed as strong in both areas, the response or likelihood of being seen as great leaders was overwhelmingly strong.

I suggest to you that there are many more strong social-skilled leaders than there are strong results-oriented leaders. By far. So today's question is: If you had only two candidates for one senior leadership position within your team and one was clearly a great people person and the other was clearly a results-oriented leader, which would you choose?

*Originally published February 14, 2014*

# DO YOU HAVE A SENSE OF HUMOUR?

I should actually start this one with a joke…

A grasshopper walks into a bar and the bartender says, "Hey – we have a drink named after you!" To which the grasshopper says, "Yeah? You have a drink called Bob?"

I love that one.

*A sense of humor is important…every day.* We all want to enjoy our work and our workplace. We want to look forward to heading out to work every day. To make this a reality, many things need to happen. Challenge, accomplishment, camaraderie, comfort and more. But it also has to be fun. As a leader, we need to create an environment that has some humor in it. Every day. If you are managing a project team, a group of BAs or a division of a large organization, this is for you. You need to find a way to lighten up the atmosphere so you hear from your colleagues that, among other things, this is a fun place to be. It can't just be "we had fun sometime last month."

*A sense of humor is important when things are* not *going well.* We are all so busy, so stressed, so nervous about our future and – in many cases – very overworked. We need to lighten up every once in a while and this is the responsibility of today's leaders – you. Great leaders will make an effort to carry a smile wherever they go and to add levity to every day. This is *not* a sign of weakness, but rather a sign of strength.

I have worked in some pretty stressful environments. Business is down and the future is not looking good. How did leadership carry this? Not well. There was very little that was fun in those offices. No smiles, no jokes, no fun. This is when a sense of humor is most important. Regardless of how bad things are going, work still has to be fun. Otherwise we run the risk of losing really good people, and when it all turns around in the future, your best people are gone. Ouch.

*A sense of humor is important when we make mistakes.* We all make mistakes. The Forbes.com article about the top attributes of leaders instructs us to "encourage your team to laugh at the mistakes instead of crying." Well said. This kind of reaction makes working for an organization worth coming to every day. We are all in this together and no one is perfect. So lighten up. Let's fix it, learn from it and not lose a good person because of it.

*A sense of humor is important when things change.* We all know people who do not handle change well. I definitely have a few in my life. When change happens and we have to go into crisis mode, we need a sense of humor. This makes the solutions easier to grasp and easier to execute.

*And finally, a sense of humor could just get you the next job.* A friend recently sent me a link to an article from Workopolis.com entitled "Infographic: Why the other person got the job, and you didn't."

"A Workopolis survey of over 300 hiring managers asked the question 'If it comes down to two job candidates with equal skills and work experience, what is the factor that will move you to hire one over the other?' The answer might surprise you. It certainly surprised us. Nearly half of respondents (45.37%) said they would choose the more enthusiastic candidate. This was followed in a distant second place by fit with the company culture, then that was followed in third place by sense of humor."

So to all of you leaders out there, I say stop being so serious every hour of every day. Come on down into the trenches and lighten up the mood. We need it. You need it.

*Originally published July 9, 2014*

# DELEGATION – A KEY TO LEADERSHIP SUCCESS

Are you able to delegate effectively?

Let's start this discussion with a look at two young companies.

1. Wedonotdelegateverywell Inc. was started by an entrepreneur who had an idea and developed the company from scratch. He was the first and only employee for the first year. Today they employ 300 people and they are growing at a rapid pace. As an employee, it looks like an exciting place to work. The trouble is that the original owner has to control everything. He is part of every decision, every idea and all of the future plans. But it works. The company is profitable and secure.

2. Weareallaboutdelegation Ltd. is also a start-up. It has the same background, but while the original owner is still there all day every day (you can't keep him away), he is a delegator. Everyone is empowered over time to take responsibility and take control of some part of the day-to-day work. The good news is that this is a personal growth opportunity. The bad news is that it is not as profitable and may not be so secure.

Where do you want to work? Of course, most of us would pick #2. Organizations that encourage responsibility, risk taking, personal growth and teamwork will be much more successful in the long run, and more important, attract better people who will stick around for a longer time.

As a leader or a manager, we need to learn how to delegate more often and with more people. This is a key management skill.

Why is delegation so important?

- *Encouragement for growth*: Delegating gives your employees or team members responsibility and authority to get work done. This creates a more productive environment, and productivity means growth for everyone.

- *Focus*: Delegating allows you to focus on what is really important. We want you to be focused on what's important for the company in the long term and not what is important today. We want you to be strategic.

- *Team*: Delegating encourages a team approach – everyone gets involved in the success of the company. This fact alone makes for a more enjoyable work environment and again a more productive business.

- *The right tool*: Delegating allows us to capitalize on others' strengths. Why not get the best-qualified people doing the work?

- *Health*: For the workaholics out there, learning how to delegate gives you an important break, and a healthier you is always good.

An article out of Rice University Executive Education entitled "Learning to Delegate" outlines: "As you move up in the organization, the managers above you watch to see not only whether you get the job done, but also how you get it done. They want to see what management skills you have, especially your ability to act strategically, with a focus on future planning and innovation. Delegating skills are essential for demonstrating that you can work at this higher level."

So why don't we delegate? Over the past 30 years, I have created numerous small entrepreneurial ventures – some staying very small but a few grew to be larger than just me. My biggest problem as an entrepreneur was delegating and my biggest excuses for *not* delegating were time and trust.

- In so many cases, I simply did not have the time to train someone, watch over them and follow up. It was way too easy just to do it myself.

- Although I'm not proud of it now, I often felt that no one could do the work as well as I could. This is a common problem for leaders. It is very difficult to give up the reigns, especially if it was your baby to begin with.

In my research, I also found other excuses for not delegating. Possibly you can identify with one of these?

- Perceived weakness: Some feel that delegating is a sign of weakness to senior managers, that those around us will think we can't do the work.

- Turf protection: If we get others to do the work, they are going to get the credit.

- Hard to give it up: You enjoy the task you are working on – it's fun.

If you are not good at delegation, you need to start today. You need to look around you and identify parts of your day-to-day activities or routines that can be assigned to others around you.

You might look seriously at the routine work you are doing and ask yourself if you are really doing it that well. I recently found myself completely overwhelmed with the details of a series of events I was running. When a few items started falling through the cracks every so often, I realized that I wasn't even very good at managing these details. It was time to delegate.

When looking for "stuff" to delegate:

- Look at the work you do that you don't do well – find someone else who can do it better.

- Find something that an employee has expressed an interest in and hand it over.

- Find work that will develop a skill that a particular employee requires.

- Look for a task that will help develop a particular employee for a future position.

The process of delegating is not to be taken lightly. You can't just wing it. You can't drop a file off on someone's desk and let them loose. You need to be very careful about how you delegate work. You need to:

- establish very clear instructions with clear deadlines.
- establish a clear level of authority and this needs to be communicated to everyone.
- establish performance expectations and behaviors.
- make sure they know how to get help and assistance.
- establish a plan – with the employee's input.
- provide required resources.
- be enthusiastic and show confidence in the person's ability.
- call regular meetings and follow-up throughout – you can't leave them out on a limb until it's too late.

And after the work has been done, spend some time with your employee to discuss lessons learned. He/she will have lots to contribute both about the task at hand and about your delegation process. This can be a good learning experience for you as well!

Delegation is important to everyone in your company: employees, you, your stakeholders, your shareholders.

Are you a good delegator?

*Originally published June 25, 2014*

# LEADERS ARE ALWAYS COMMITTED

The sixth key leadership trait according to *Forbes* magazine is commitment. I have been trying to think about leadership without commitment. I can't. They simply cannot exist without each other.

Have you ever decided to leave a company and be faced with the dreaded two weeks or so until you really physically leave? This is a dead zone. Your commitment has gone. Without commitment, you are dead to the organization.

Commitment is all about the drive to make something work. A relationship, a business and even yourself.

BusinessAnalystTimes.com published an article on September 30, 2015 entitled "The Five Commitments of Leadership" by Mark Leheney. Leheney lists the five commitments as:

- To the self: how much you work on developing yourself as a human being, to be the best leader you can be. In fact, it is self-awareness that is the first major step toward becoming truly committed.
- To people: how much you really focus on connecting with those around you in order to work effectively with them.
- To the organization: how much you are devoted to the intentions and performance of the place where you work so that you show up with maximum energy and conviction.
- To the truth: how much you tell and invite the truth, even when it is hard, in order to keep yourself, others and the organization on a right course.

- To leadership: how much you answer a call to lead and choose to engage in proven, effective leadership behaviors.

As a leader, you are constantly under a watchful eye by your employees and your team. Your commitment to the organization, the brand and all of your people is always right up front. If it slips, weakens or goes away, the audience will see it immediately.

You need to be committed – day in and day out.

According to the *Forbes* article, "If you expect your team to work hard and produce quality content, you're going to need to lead by example. There is no greater motivation than seeing the boss down in the trenches working alongside everyone else, showing that hard work is being done on every level."

Peter Drucker, the founder of modern management, said: "Unless commitment is made, there are only promises and hopes…but no plans."

So every day we need to look in the mirror and confirm our commitment. If the answer is at all gray or wavering, we need to stop and address the reasons why. Possibly a short-term period of questioning – easy to fix. Maybe a few days of looking for greener pastures – hopefully short term. Maybe something is not going our way. Time will heal that one.

But in any case, if we have tried to fix the situation and we are still not committed, it is time to make a big adjustment. Maybe even time to move on. A great leader will see this clearly and make the right move.

Commitment is one of the keys to great leadership. Without it, you are lost.

As Forbes.com puts it: "By proving your commitment to the brand and your role, you will not only earn the respect of your team, but will also instill that same hardworking energy among your staff."

*Originally published July 23, 2014*

# SIX THINGS YOU CAN DO TODAY TO PREPARE FOR LEADERSHIP TOMORROW

Many of us are in what I call a pre-leadership position. We are in a role where we are managing people and making mid-level decisions on projects and initiatives that are important to the health and success of our organizations. Generally, we are looking forward to a future as a senior leader – here or elsewhere.

If you know me, or have heard me present, or been a regular reader of this blog, you might know that I often refer to our professional strategic plan: a process that creates an action plan for our professional future. Within the plan, we will find action items to get us from "here" to "there."

So what if we are managing today and want to become leaders tomorrow? What should I find in the list of action items in my professional strategic plan?

1. *Knock your responsibilities out of the park.* In everything you do, do it beyond expectations. Kill it – day in and day out. This level of performance will get recognized by your managers, your peers and especially the leaders in your current organization. This is one of the most important traits of any future leader. Show your stripes now.

2. *Help your boss succeed.* My father-in-law used to say: "Make heroes out of everyone around you." You do not have to be the star attraction to get recognized. The supporting role is often the more important and – many times – the most rewarded.

3. *Seize leadership opportunities, no matter how small.* Act on anything you can to practice being a leader. Events, presentations, marketing campaigns, new product launches – anything. You won't be left out there alone, hopefully. Use the experience to learn and to explore your new skills.

4. *Don't be a jerk.* Jerks complain a lot but don't contribute to any solutions. Jerks make life miserable for others and put your organization's reputation at risk with behavior that is unacceptable. Jerks don't believe in teamwork and don't believe that paying it forward has any merits. Don't go there.

5. *Find role models.* Find people who you want to emulate, who are doing what you want to do in the future or who stand out as examples of the kind of leader you want to be. If you know them personally, foster that relationship, feed it, nurture it and make lots of notes. If they are a public personality and inaccessible in person, read everything they write, watch them on YouTube and on TED Talks and attend any event that gets you closer to their thoughts, ideas and dreams.

6. *Build relationships.* Now. Not later. Connect with key people in your life on a regular basis. Set dates in your calendar to touch base every few months. Find new relationships that might be able to connect you to key people some day in the future or who are authorities in their own right. The relationships in your professional life are probably the most important asset you have. Now is the time, when you don't need it, to seek out and establish your professional support system so that it is there for you when you really do need it.

The *Harvard Business Review* (Fall 2014) outlined: "If you want to become a leader, don't wait for the fancy title or the corner office. You can begin to act, think and communicate like a leader long before that promotion. Even if you're still several levels down and someone else is calling all the shots, there are numerous ways to demonstrate your potential and carve your path to the role you want."

Are you planting the seeds today for your new leadership position tomorrow?
*Originally published May 13, 2015*

# CONFIDENCE CARRIES THE DAY

The fifth key leadership trait according to *Forbes* magazine is confidence. The magazine outlined: "As the leader, by staying calm and confident, you will help keep the team feeling the same."

As I think about my professional/entrepreneurial career and those "few" dark days of panic, frustration and fear, I always remembered the need to stay confident. And it sure wasn't easy. I struggled often to put on a brave face in front of the troops or even my family at times. But I knew that if I lost my confidence, my "people" would lose their confidence in me. And that spells trouble. I got us here. I can't lose hope. I have to stay strong and I have to believe in the original plan.

Confidence is one of those emotions that we can't hide. I am actually not sure if there is a scenario when you would want to hide it but I do know that everyone is watching or listening. They will see the cracks.

Francisco Dao wrote in *Inc* magazine: "Self-confidence is the fundamental basis from which leadership grows. Trying to teach leadership without first building confidence is like building a house on a foundation of sand. It may have a nice coat of paint, but it is ultimately shaky at best."

We need to be confident to make decisions. Confidence allows us to make decisions quickly and decisively. No waffling. No second-guessing. The best of us will listen to everyone and everything first and weigh the options. But then we will pull the trigger and make the decision.

Some people out there will respond quickly to all of this and say: "What happens if you're wrong?" Well, then, I am wrong. I will admit it and move on. Yes, if I am wrong more often than right, I will lose my position. But for many of us, this is the risk we take as leaders, entrepreneurs or just plain old "doers."

The most confident of us are very willing to be wrong once in a while. Confidence allows us to be wrong because we know we will be right the next time. Move on.

Your confidence builds confidence all around you. If you look and sound confident, everyone around you will step into line and join in your confidence. Your confidence breeds others' confidence.

Confidence shows in our manners, speech and presence, both physically and – even these days – electronically. As I walk into a conference room to give a speech, I need to look confident in all ways. It is that first impression. The whole audience is looking at me before I step onto the podium. I had better look confident.

Today, we have electronic profiles: Facebook, LinkedIn, Twitter and more. Even here we need to look confident. The written profile, the biography, the photos. They all communicate confidence (or lack thereof).

Your customers and suppliers want to see your confidence. So often their success is in some way tied to your success. You are a part of next quarter's revenue numbers. Or you are the source of a service that they really need or want. If you are not confident in what you do, you will lose them fast. Many of us will jump early from a sinking ship.

So, for many reasons, a leader of any sort needs to be confident. You are good at what you do. Your organization is good at what it does. People like you, want to work for you and want to ride your success.

Embrace it every day.
*Originally published July 14, 2014*

# ARE YOU EMOTIONALLY FIT?

Forbes.com published an article called "5 Ways To Transform Yourself Into A Leader" in which it suggested that leaders need emotional fitness. How true.

We look up to our leaders for all types of inspiration and guidance. We need our leaders to hold strong in times of chaos, during the ups and downs of business and through general day-to-day stress. If a leader panics, everyone else will.

Leaders who panic will send signals right through the organization, and the team will soon be in panic mode as well. Says Forbes.com: "Leaders tap into an inner Buddha, an unwavering stillness that empowers them to take a deep breath and keep moving forward."

I like that. "Take a deep breath and keep moving forward." Lost deals, lost customers, lost production time due to equipment failure, accidents, personal tragedies and more. They all require a steady hand, a steady heart and calmness throughout.

Finding that level of emotional fitness cannot be easy. I think it requires a deep-down belief that nothing that happens will ultimately end the world. Sounds funny, but sometimes I think that as long as I have my health, my family and my friends, I will be alright. As long as I can say that I gave it my very best effort and did everything I could, to the best of my ability, then I would be alright.

It is easy for me to remain calm if I think that I will be fine in the end. But what about everyone else? If the panic could very well lead to unemployment for many, then it must be hard to show calmness before the end.

But even in extreme cases like this, calmness must prevail. A leader is not going to get high marks for panicking as the ship goes down. He/she will get marks for compassion, understanding and never leaving the ship in its worst time.

Emotional fitness. Calm, cool and collected at the best and worst of times.

Are you emotionally fit?

*Originally published May 6, 2015*

# THE TOP 10 QUALITIES THAT MAKE A GREAT LEADER

I have been working through an article from Forbes.com that listed the top 10 qualities that make a great leader.

They were:

1. Honesty
2. The ability to delegate
3. Communication
4. A sense of humor
5. Confidence
6. Commitment
7. Positive attitude
8. Creativity
9. Intuition
10. The ability to inspire

I thought it might be interesting to look back at the activity on each posting and see which ones interested my readers the most.

Before I hit the statistics page of my website, I looked at this list and thought through my top 10 list.

For me, the key to leadership success has to lie in communication. A recent review by the Schulich Executive Education Centre in Toronto suggests that the top two requirements in senior management education were leadership and communication. If you do not have a good strong "communication engine" within the organization and at the top of the organization, you put everyone and everything at risk.

A strong communication engine ensures that everyone is in the loop, that misunderstandings are minimized, that key stakeholders are kept aware, that employees know where they are going and why – and the list goes on. So much of what we see that goes wrong in today's organizations can be attributed to poor communications.

Which blog posts attracted the most interest from my readers? Note that this is not necessarily the trait that my readers thought most important – just most interesting and thus the most read.

The results (percentage of total hits):

| | |
|---|---|
| The ability to delegate | 16.72% |
| Confidence | 15.74% |
| A sense of humor | 15.49% |
| Communication | 8.70% |
| Creativity | 8.33% |
| Positive attitude | 8.27% |
| Honesty | 7.96% |
| The ability to inspire | 6.74% |
| Intuition | 6.12% |
| Commitment | 5.94% |

If you see a blog post cross your desk on a Wednesday around 2 p.m., what is going to attract you to read it? If the post were about something you knew well and were good at, would you open it? Nope. But if it were on a topic that promised to fill a gap or help you as a leader in some way, you would open it.

So from these numbers, I would suggest that the leadership trait that most interested us and that possibly we felt most in need of understanding better is the ability to delegate. This makes sense. I think leaders do have a hard time at this. We so often think we can do it better or faster if we just do it ourselves. This is especially true of new leaders or middle-management leaders. Giving up the reigns is hard. And it is good news that many of us know that this is an issue. Of all the posts that discuss the Forbes.com list of top 10 leadership traits, this is the one you open the most.

If you haven't read it, have a look: http://davidbarrett.ca/key-leadership-trait-2-ability-delegate.

*Originally published September 3, 2014*

# 4 STEPS TO BECOMING MORE RESILIENT

I recently heard a popular leader referred to as "tough as nails." She is famous for finding a way out of difficult situations – gracefully and unscathed.

As leaders, we often discover that something has gone terribly wrong and our reaction – in the short, medium and long term – will often define us for years to come. As a leader or manager, you need to make a decision fast – tackle this adversity head-on. As leaders, we need to be able to react to adverse situations quickly and decisively.

We need to stop, analyze the situation very carefully, both internally and externally, and make some very tough decisions.

Tough as nails? Or resilient? I think resilient.

Most dictionaries define psychological resilience as "an individual's ability to properly adapt to stress and adversity".

Rebecca Shambaugh, in her book *Leadership Secrets of Hillary Clinton*, says: "We need the ability to keep moving ahead, no matter what obstacles we meet, overcoming and thriving on adversity. Leaders must be looking ahead, seeing the possibilities, and then connecting with the hearts and minds of followers to engage them in a new vision." Resilience has been identified as Hillary Clinton's key strength as she moves toward the Democratic nomination for U.S. President in 2016.

Being tough as nails is a characteristic or a trait. We use the words to describe an element of personality that is relatively stable and typical of that person.

Being resilient is less an ingrained characteristic and more a quality that can be taught, mentored or coached. Very different.

So how do we become more resilient?

Step 1: Understand that this is a science – this is something that can be taught, coached or mentored.

Step 2: Call this the "as is" state. Understand your core values – what you stand for in the business world or your personal life. What makes you tick and what makes you ticked off. This baseline is essential to your journey.

Step 3: From the baseline above, list the typical stresses, problems and difficult situations that you commonly face.

Step 4: Address the different ways you might deal with these scenarios – being sure they line up with your core values. Rehearse the different responses, practice, review options and consult others.

The key to becoming more resilient is to treat the journey as a science and not an art. The key is to realize that you cannot wing it when it comes to responding to adversity.

Develop an internal process for dealing with stress and obstacles and fine-tune the responses over time.

*Originally published August 12, 2015*

# MANAGING

# CAN YOU TALK CXO LANGUAGE?

If you want to become a leader in your organization, you need to be able to talk CxO language. The executives (CEO, CIO, COO, CFO, etc.) in our organizations are looking for leaders who can communicate with them at their level.

As we mature within our organizations, the work we do will lead us closer and closer to what we call the C-Suite – the executive level of our organization. There will come a day when we need to communicate to our executives or maybe even the board of directors about something that we are working on.

As with any dialogue with anyone in our lives, if we don't talk the same language, the task at hand is extremely difficult.

My friend Gary Heerkens out of Rochester, NY, includes this language requirement in his chapter of the book I published with Derek Vigar *The Keys to Our Success* (and is featured in my keynote presentation by the same name) when he talks about the importance of being business-savvy. Step 1 of understanding the big picture is to understand the language of the people managing the big picture.

I'm getting better at communicating with my nine-month-old granddaughter. I'm learning her language. It took me too many years to learn the language of my teenage son and daughters. Last week I presented to an audience of software and systems-quality managers. To be successful, which I think I was, I needed to understand even just a small part of their language. Last week I struggled to learn the language of bridge at my first lesson.

So what's CxO language?

- Income statement
- Balance sheet
- Cash flow statement
- Cost-benefit analysis
- Return on investment (ROI)
- Internal rate of return (IRR)
- Current vs fixed assets
- Long-term vs short-term liabilities

The C-Suite thinks daily about the success of a company – at all levels and from many angles. But the most important key to success for them is the bottom line.

If you understand this, two things will happen: your dialogue with them becomes easier and you will be recognized as someone who "gets it."

If this language is foreign to you or makes you uncomfortable and if you aspire to a senior position within your organization, you need to learn how to talk this talk.

The solution is not an executive MBA. It is not three years of night school for accountants. It could simply be a three-day course on financial management for non-financial managers. Two to three days on how to read a balance sheet and a profit-and-loss statement, how to calculate return on investment, how do create a cash flow statement. It could be an online program that will guide you through the fundamentals at your own pace. It could even be a coach or tutor you can employ to get you over this hump. But you do need to get over this hump.

Remember, you do not need to learn how to be an accountant. You need to understand the "stuff" that accountants produce. This is the "stuff" that feeds the bottom line and this is what keeps our C-Suite up at night.

Understanding this language will do three things for you and your career:

1. You will stand out from others around you.

2. Your conversations with senior management and executives will be much easier and interesting.
3. Your path to a senior leadership position will be significantly easier to navigate.

Can you talk the CxO language?

- (Gain on investment – cost of investment) / cost of investment = ?
- Assets – liabilities = ?
- $FV / (1 + r)^n = ?$ (sorry)

*Originally published February 3, 2014*

# HONESTY AND INTEGRITY – KEY FOR ALL OF US

I am thinking about the key elements of good and great leadership and the management of people. There are many. Google the top 10 traits of great leaders and you will find 20 to 30 unique traits over numerous lists.

Honesty and integrity. These two words appear on everyone's list. Samuel Johnson is quoted as saying, "The first step toward greatness is to be honest."

Over my years in business, for myself and for others, I was often challenged by a decision I had to make regarding a course of action, a conversation or a plan. I had to decide between door #1 and door #2. Each was legal and aboveboard. But one door would lead me into a space that I would question or feel ever so slightly guilty about. In one case, I wouldn't tell the whole truth but the results favored me over someone else. In another case, one of the options would mean that I would always know that I got the deal only by slightly altering the truth about a competitor. And then there was the day that I had the option of cutting a big corner to get a job done – knowing that it would be years until anyone noticed but that I would be long gone by then.

Many people will look at ethics and honesty as gray areas as opposed to black and white. This is a mistake. There is nothing gray about being ethical and honest. These people will tell you that we are all sinners – it's just a matter of scale. No. The decisions we make every day land on one side or the other – never on the fence.

As the beacon of your team, your company, your division, people will look to you as an example. Cut the corner, make an exception, act slightly unethically and they will *all* take note.

And without honesty and integrity, there is no trust.

Jim Clemmer is a writer on all things about leadership. In a recent post for GoArticles.com, he wrote: "Honesty and integrity are motherhood leadership phrases. And they should be. They are fundamental to leadership. Honesty and integrity produce trust, which produces high levels of confidence. High confidence encourages people to dream and to reach for new horizons. High confidence fosters risk-taking. Risk-taking and initiative are fundamental to organization change and improvement."

Our ability to lead others is directly related to our ability to forge strong relationships. Strong relationships are dependent upon trust. Trust provides the glue.

As a leader of a team or group or a whole company, we are being asked to communicate information about many things. Strategy, results, plans, deals and more. Some of us will look at the details of the brief and think about twisting the information ever so slightly in order to hide or exaggerate something. No one will know.

A recent survey by The Discovery Group of Sharon and Wellfleet, MA, a company specializing in employee-opinion surveys, found that 52% of employees don't believe the information they receive from management. Misinformation festers a lack of trust. It will infiltrate all parts of the business going forward. Can you believe that 5don't believe what management says!

This highlights an important point. Honesty is not just telling the truth. It is just as much about telling all of the truth. Holding back information or even hiding information will eventually catch up to us. Trust, gone. The power of your leadership, gone.

As a great leader, you need to set an example for everyone around you. You need to establish a standard of behavior that includes how you communicate, how you act, how you react and how you interact.

Jack Zenger is a regular contributor to *Forbes* magazine. On May 17, 2012, he posted:

> Our ability and courage to speak honestly with one another is most certainly at the heart of treating one another with respect. Indeed our research on this leadership quality of integrity paints an interesting picture. We found that leaders who received high scores on honesty and integrity also received high scores on the following five behaviors:
> 1. Approachable
> 2. Acted with humility
> 3. Listened with great intensity
> 4. Made decisions carefully
> 5. Acted assertively

Trust, leadership and integrity all lead to other key traits of great leaders. A great career needs a strong foundation of honesty.

*Originally published June 18, 2014*

# WHEN WAS THE LAST TIME YOU DID AN OFFICE WALK-ABOUT?

If you are a manager at any level, a leader or even a coordinator of a group of people, you should be doing what is sometimes referred to as a regular walkabout. What is this? A walkabout is time spent walking among, and connecting with, your team or employees. This is a set time, maybe an hour a week, with no agenda – just a time to connect at any level with the folks who work for you.

Our employees today want to feel connected at work. They want to be a part of a community that is interesting, challenging and even fun. But as well, they need to feel connected in some way to their managers and leaders. Without this connection, they might begin to feel that no one cares, no one is paying attention and no one would know if there were troubles in their lives or work.

A regular, if not weekly, walkabout among your team is vital to making this connection. It will help to identify unhappiness, personal or professional issues, important milestones in employees' lives and more. This is the part of our relationship with our team that can make a difference between long-term happy employees and high-turnover unhappy employees.

An important distinction here: this is an opportunity to take an interest in people personally, but not to become personally connected. There is a difference and – as a leader and manager – this is important.

Your walkabout should be a regularly scheduled, diarized event in your weekly calendar. Otherwise it will definitely fall from your list of priorities the first or second round. The time you set aside depends on the size of your team. You don't have to speak to everyone but you definitely have to show your face to everyone.

I was running a leadership workshop last week where we were discussing what great leaders do in the first three weeks of their jobs. One attendee commented that their company recently acquired a new executive leader. The first three days were great as she met everyone and made a great effort to connect with as many people as possible. That was the good news. The bad news was that they never saw her again. Buried in an office with lots to do. That's no excuse. Your priority must be regular connection with your team.

Depending on your ability to remember a lot of detail about a lot of people, you should be employing a science to this walkabout. My memory is lousy, so after my walkabouts, I record information that is important to those relationships that I've just touched. Pending events like weddings or babies, past or future holiday travels, health issues and more. If I hear of an upcoming event, I will diarize a follow-up conversation on a future walkabout. Some may say that this applied science makes it phony but I don't care. People genuinely appreciate my interest regardless of how much science I applied to it.

If you know me well, you will know that I have a birthday call list in my life. These are phone calls (not emails, not text messages, not Facebook comments) that I make throughout the year to people in my life. Family, friends, staff, coworkers are all on the list. The recipients love the call. I love the call because it allows me to touch base with some very important people in my life. But I don't "wing" this process. All of these calls are diarized annually and I am reminded 24 hours prior to each call. (I love technology.) No one cares how I remember to call them. They just appreciate the call.

If you need to cover more people than you have time for, then put your groups on a rotation basis. Schedule the different teams each week. Read your notes before you return to the team. Make a point of following up on some of the conversations you had when you spoke to them last. Note the people you missed the last time that you might want to connect with this time.

Regardless of whether you apply a science to this or not, taking an interest in the personal and professional lives of your team members in this casual approach is vital to a happy and engaged team.

Take one hour a week, shut down your life, relax and interact with your team. You will be amazed at what you learn and you will be amazed at the reaction of the audience. This is a win-win for all of us.

When was the last time you did an office walkabout?

*Originally published January 21, 2015*

# MANAGING EXPECTATIONS

As leader, project manager or team coordinator, you instinctively want to deliver well and please everyone. And everyone on your team wants to do the same thing. We are all trying to please each other. It's natural. We expect success. Why would anyone start off in a project expecting failure?

We are very good at setting expectations at the front end. This is easy. We will deliver on time, on budget and within the defined scope.

But we can't always deliver as promised. Things change. Budgets, timing, environments and more. The original expectation of our customers, stakeholders, team and others are no longer valid.

So when the change hits, what do you do? Who do you call first? What do you do to manage the expectations of all of the stakeholders?

Managing expectations is one of the most important keys to our success as project managers and leaders.

Some might say it's easy. Aim low – deliver high. Perfectly simple. But this approach won't last long. The smart people out there will begin to realize that they are being fooled. I think setting expectations is all about trust, communication and honesty.

As things change, everything we agreed to, or promised, is at risk. This is the moment the true leaders shine. We need to confront change immediately. We need to communicate to everyone involved. Their expectations must be adjusted immediately. But more important, we need to get everyone onside so that the changes required are agreed on early and implemented quickly.

I tell anyone I work with, or who works for me, to keep talking to me. Tell me how you are doing. Tell me if you think it will be late, or over budget, or the wrong color or not quite as promised. Set my expectations correctly as soon as you can. And feel free to reset my expectations as required. I know we aren't all perfect. I know that we will make mistakes. I know that things will happen above and beyond our control. But I want to know about it as soon as possible – not at the 11th hour. Please. This way, you see, I can help, or get others to help. And at a minimum, I can adjust my own stakeholders' expectations.

This is the key to project success. If the original plan has to be adjusted, this is fine. The earlier, the better. And the earlier we get at it, the better chance that the new plan becomes *the* plan. The bottom line is that no one wants to be surprised. No one.

Plan the work and work the plan and find a simple, easy way to keep everyone in the project on top of the progress. No surprises.

*Originally published April 30, 2014*

# ARE YOU PRACTICING 'GOOD MEETINGS'?

Do people leave your meetings saying "That was a really valuable use of my time" or "What a great meeting!"? Or do you hear "What a waste of time" as they are walking out the door?

It is so easy to bash meetings: a waste of time, poorly organized, a lousy chair, no real purpose, out of control.

A company called Meeting King of Tolland, CT surveyed their customers and discovered that:

- 37% of employee time is spent in meetings.
- 47% consider too many meetings the biggest waste of time.
- 39% of meeting participants admitted to dozing off during a meeting.
- more than 70% brought other work to meetings.

But why just bash meetings? Why not fix them?

Great meetings can be very worthwhile, valuable and important to the cause. The same survey found that "92% of meeting attendees value meetings as an opportunity to contribute to the organization."

So how do we "do" good meetings?   In my mind, there are four major components to good meetings:

1.  A good foundation
2.  Purpose
3.  Structure
4.  Measurement

A good foundation means that we are going to meet with all the right pieces in place: people, facility, food, documentation and technology. The first 10 minutes of a meeting is not the time to realize that you don't have the key people involved. Meetings are not for wasting other people's time and energy when they really don't need to be there. Early-morning meetings require coffee. Meetings between noon and 1 p.m. require lunch. The facility needs to be the right size, all required documentation needs to be available during the meeting and you need to make sure that your technology works. A solid foundation will position the rest of the meeting for success.

Purpose means that we all know why we are in the meeting. Too many meetings waste too much time because we really don't need to meet. Every meeting should have a declared and stated purpose, and every attendee should know why they are there.

Structure is more about the mechanics of the meeting: a chairperson, a scribe and a timekeeper. An agenda that is distributed ahead of time, that we follow and that we stay on top of. Minutes from previous meetings are reviewed at the beginning and not at the end of each meeting. Ground rules or terms of engagement on which we all agree: respect for people's time and opinions, timeliness and more. Your agenda should include all questions that need to be addressed in the meeting.

Measurement means that we go back and ask ourselves and others if the meeting did what it was supposed to do. This ideally is addressed before we adjourn the meeting. It always brings back the purpose of the meeting and reminds us that we weren't there just to waste our time and that we had a purpose in mind. Some people might take the second step and ask how we could have spent the time any better.

We need to stop wasting our time and the time of others. Our meetings should be purposeful, well run and efficient. They should have a goal in mind and everybody involved should be able to benefit from the time spent. Anything short of this is an example of bad meeting practices.

Is it time you looked at your meetings and asked yourself, or others, how you are doing?

Are you practicing good meetings?

*Originally published April 15, 2015*

# 6 WAYS TO BETTER TIME MANAGEMENT FOR ALL LEADERS

I had a friend in my life a while back who was heading up a very large corporation in Winnipeg and living in Toronto. Every Monday he would hop in the car and drive to Pearson International Airport, fly to Winnipeg and live and work there for the week. Each Friday afternoon he would fly home and spend the weekend with his family. And if that weren't enough, he would spend three to four days a week flying around the country visiting other offices. I often wondered how he could pull this off with all the work commitments during the week plus the traveling plus his family plus keeping his own health in check.

The fact is, great leaders need to be great time managers. They need to have the ability to manage the distinct sections of their lives throughout the days and weeks. The leader who wakes up every day and "wings it" will not be a great leader for long.

Time management is a very personal thing. Some of us think in terms of a week while others think in terms of a day. Some use a hard copy diary system while others use technology. Personally I am a technology guy (Google calendars + Remember the Milk), and when I manage my time, I think in terms of one day. For me, my day involves six steps.

1. Start your day prepared. I never wake up to a new day without being prepared. I will rework my to-do list, check over my calendar and plot my priorities for that day. In my case, I find that without preparation I'm often panicking during the evening and losing sleep over things that I may not have control over. If just for my health, this preparation phase is vitally important.

2. Deal with the top 20% issues. We all know about the 20/80 rule. We so easily get pulled in by the 80% of our work that isn't as important. In our preparation phase, our prioritization needs to address the top issues of the day or the week. My top 20% items always sit at the top of my action list for the day and I schedule the time to deal with them. The 80% stuff will fill in the blanks of the day.

3. Deal with the big picture. Leaders need to take time out of their day to look at the big picture, to address the strategy and be reminded of the vision. Strategy execution is not easy and not done very well. There are many reasons for this but one of them is that leaders have trouble focusing on strategy as they deal with the day-to-day issues. Leaders need to take time to refocus on where we need them most – the big picture. At least a part of the day anyway.

4. Sometimes we are so busy that we only engage with the key people around us for days on end. This is a mistake. As busy as leaders can get, we need to connect to the outside world: customers, suppliers, employees, friends and family. Stay connected and manage our connections daily.

5. Take personal time. Our health is the most important part of everything we do. Without it, our organizations won't have us around for long. Our families will not have us around for long. Leadership brings stress, and stress can bring serious health issues. Work out every day if possible, meditate and take time to relax and reenergize, if only for 20 minutes mid-afternoon. Staying healthy is critical to great leadership and we need to take personal time to look after this part of our life.

6. How was your day? Did you accomplish what you wanted? Did you deal with the 20% issues? Did you visit the big picture? Did you call or visit or write to someone in your world? And did you do something for you and your health? This daily scorecard is a way that we can stay on top of the priorities in our life – both personal and professional. Leaders need to be good time managers. Are you?

*Originally published April 22, 2015*

# HOW DO YOU HANDLE THE TOUGH TIMES?

Life doesn't always go as planned. In business, we need to be ready for the unexpected, the rough times and the disasters.

I am talking about anything from a short-term power failure that lasts a few hours to a market crash. I am talking about a short-term glitch in your computer system to the long-term effect of a bad decision by your company.

Short or long term, big or small, rough times in our business, within our team, in our own jobs are a reality that most of us cannot avoid. The true test is how we handle the rough times.

For leaders, these are the times that call for the carefully worded response, the very public reaction, the special approach to employees, the new crisis management strategy and more.

Whatever happened is history and that cannot be changed. What happens going forward is all in your hands. And as leaders, you can be sure that everyone is watching. Your response to the situation will set the tone across the whole organization or department or team. It is vital that you approach this phase carefully, strategically and sensitively.

Doug Boebinger wrote a chapter in the book I wrote with Derek Vigar, *The Keys to Our Success – Lessons Learned from 25 of Our Best Project Managers*, in which he talks about "Black Swan Theory." Black swans are very-low-probability events that have a very high impact: war, disease outbreak, terrorist attacks, a financial meltdown.

We need to expect the unexpected. But often we don't. We are never really prepared for the unexpected.

For some of us, the first reaction is to find the cause and lay blame. This is a natural reaction. If you have control, you need to stop the flood. But if you have no control, then you need to move on immediately. Laying blame needs to wait. The last thing a leader should do now is look for someone to blame.

From this moment, your reactions are on center stage.

For me, five words come to mind: calm, fast, sensitive, open and visible.

1. Calm: Anything else sends the wrong message and affects everyone else's state.

2. Fast: Your reaction and actions must be decisive and quick. Time is typically not in long supply and every minute or hour counts.

3. Sensitive: Be sensitive to the states of mind of your employees or team, and to the fear that many feel about the near and long-term future of their jobs or even their health.

4. Open: To collaborative participation by your team, advisors and others. Now is the time to listen carefully, take in all advice and accept help from many.

5. Visible: Be visible to everyone around you and beyond. No hiding. Talk to your team, communicating with everyone regularly to show your concern and involvement.

The hardest part about reacting to the rough times or a disaster is that it requires an approach that may not be normal for you and this is exactly what will define you as a great leader. Dial up the parts of your leadership style that you need now and dial down the parts that are not going to fit at this moment. Drop the regular day-to-day approach to your business and do what is needed now.

The rough times could be around the corner and a disaster could be around the corner. How prepared are you? How will you react to these times?

*Originally published October 1, 2014*

# 5 THINGS I LEARNED ABOUT ORGANIZATIONAL CHANGE MANAGEMENT

I recently hosted a gathering of senior resources from local banks, insurance companies, retail organizations and others that we call the "Enterprise Project Management Office Executive Forum", held at the Schulich Executive Education Centre, York University, in Toronto.

This is a monthly gathering of people interested in topics pertaining to enterprise project issues. Today's meeting was about organizational change management (OCM). Now, I must admit that I wasn't, by any stretch, the expert in the room. In fact, far from it. That's why I invited my friend Lesa Berec to present and facilitate the ongoing discussion.

Here is what I learned today about organizational change management.

1. *It's complicated.* What is OCM? Where does it belong? Who is responsible? Is it a part of our project management life cycle or a separate stream completely independent? Is it so important? These are all questions that today's attendees are struggling with now or have struggled with in parts of their organizations in the not-so-distant past. It's complicated because, even if a few of us figured it all out, it is still hard to sell it in the field. (This sounded a lot to me like project management in IT back in 1997!) It's complicated because we are dealing with varying degrees of misunderstanding, lack of interest and/or a lack of education.

2. *Change management needs to be tied to business benefits.* Stakeholder satisfaction, user adaption and ROI are all key components to change management. And these are all business benefits. Change can be sold and

promoted only when it is tied directly to business benefits. Change without this connection does not work.

3. *Everyone needs to understand it and buy in.* I love the phrase "the key is to know what you don't know" and this is exactly what one of the organization's leaders said as they rolled out OCM training to every project manager and business analyst. Just one to two days. They don't need to be experts but they do need to understand it.

And then the executive sponsors. A half-day for every one of them! How to be a sponsor? What is expected from them? What should they expect from project managers and everything they need to understand about OCM!

And then the executive team. They really don't get it either. Honestly. One of our participants quoted a Forbes survey that suggested that more executives are fired for their inability to manage change than for any other reason. Everyone needs to understand.

4. *Change management belongs in the business.* For OCM to work, it needs to start with and stay with the business side of the house and not IT. The business establishes business benefits, assesses the risks and establishes the portfolio of work to be done.

5. *Change management cannot be a separate stream from the project methodology.* It needs to be embedded from the start to the finish and beyond. It should start at the strategic plan or at least at the portfolio development. Get the sponsor on board right at the outset and make OCM a part of the whole life cycle of the project. And very important, change management teams need a position of authority within the project life cycle.

This is what I learned today about organizational change management. It was a great meeting and a real education for me. Are you a change management disciple? I am thinking you might want to be.
*Originally published November 26, 2014*

# PERSONAL

# HAVE YOU STARTED YOUR 2015 PERSONAL STRATEGIC PLAN?

As the year 2014 came to a close, my wife and I sat down and started the process of revisiting our personal strategic plan. This is something that we've been doing for a number of years. We both find the exercise rewarding, revealing and very productive.

For the two of us, this is an in-depth look at certain parts of our lives, both individually and as a 'team'. This is our analysis of our current state of affairs and our plan for the future.

In business, we are always creating or dealing with a strategic plan. This is an essential tool for any organization. It creates the road map, going forward, of where we want to be and how we are going to get there. This is exactly what your personal strategic plan can do for you.

Many of us will start the New Year with a New Year's resolution(s): exercise more, work more, work less, go on a special vacation. Your personal strategic plan is an extension to this thought process. It actually forces you to put a plan in place to execute the desired outcome.

Quite honestly, if our lives are static and never changing, a personal strategic plan would be a waste of time. But I struggle to find anyone in my life where this is the case. Our lives are constantly bringing us change and this requires a plan to manage the process and the outcome. The looming retirement years, children heading out to college or university, a new family on the way, a new home, a change of career. There are so many things that will challenge our lives and require us to be organized, focused and have an end goal in sight.

In my life, the process of creating a short- or long-term plan with my wife has paid dividends many times over. A major change in our financial position, the first year as empty nesters, the ever-approaching retirement years, our health, our plans for staying in touch with special friends and more. Each of these areas has brought, or will bring, big changes to our lives. We need a plan.

A personal strategic plan will address any, or all, of the key areas of your life that are important or strategic to you today: health, finances, social life, spiritual life, recreation, professional life and more. In each case, the formula is the same.

Step 1. *Where are you now?* What is the current state of your health or finances or whatever else you're dealing with? In the business world, this is where we apply our SWOT analysis: strength, weaknesses, opportunities, threats. A little bit of an overkill on the personal side but an interesting part of the equation if you want to go there.

Step 2. *Where do you want to be in the future?* Six months out, one year out or even three and five years out, if you wish. This is the opportunity to dream or deal with reality and face the coming years.

Step 3. *How are you going to get there?* What needs to happen in order for you to be where you want to be in the future?

There are two key ingredients to all of this:

1. *Do it.* Actually sitting down and focusing on the selected areas of your life and creating a current state, future state and a plan. If you are working with a partner, consider doing this over a nice dinner or glass of wine or during a long drive.

2. *Revisit it.* Diarizing six months or one year down the road to pull out the document and read it to yourself or to your partner. Honestly, without this second piece, the first is useless. You need to measure and hold yourself accountable. This step serves to remind you every six months or

so how important this whole process is.

My personal strategic plan addresses all aspects of my life but not all to the same detail. In some cases, the analysis is short and simple and may not need a plan going forward. But other parts will need a lot deeper analysis and a fairly detailed plan.

For the parts of the plan that deal with me only, I find that it is important to have a partner to hear me out and to listen to my analysis. Someone to whom I can be accountable. The other parts that involve both of us are always a joint effort in analysis, planning and execution.

If you have started your personal strategic plan or – better yet – completed it, congratulations! If this is new to you, then it may be time to pick a few of your life "departments" and build a plan.

Good luck. Let's chat again about this next year and see how you did.

*Originally published January 7, 2015*

# EVERYONE SHOULD HAVE A VISION

I used to tell myself that I need a plan. Without a plan, how can you achieve your goals?

But I should also have been asking about my goals – what is my vision of the future? You need a clear vision of where you are headed in order to come up with a plan.

The key ingredient to success, professionally and personally, is the presence of a vision.

We all need a vision – a picture of where we want to be at some point of time in the future. It really doesn't matter how clear or colorful or large or small it is. It just needs to be there. The vision will drive the plan. The plan drives the team, the work, the money and more.

Maybe there is some confusion between the vision statement and the vision I am trying to define here. Maybe I am using the wrong term.

The vision I am talking about answers the questions:

- What do you want to be when you grow up?
- Where do you want to be in three years?
- Where will your company be in five years?

These questions are not answered by a vision statement as we all know the term.

"PepsiCo's responsibility is to continually improve all aspects of the world in which we operate – environment, social, economic – creating a better tomorrow than today. Our vision is put into action through programs and a focus on environmental stewardship, activities to benefit society, and a commitment to build shareholder value by making PepsiCo a truly sustainable company."

Nice vision statement but not what I am looking for. If I asked Indra Nooyi, the current CEO of PepsiCo, what her vision for the company was, I don't think I would get the statement above. I would hope to hear about share price, company growth goals and organization milestones.

If I asked my daughter where she wants to be in three years' time, I am looking for her vision – her desired state in three years. I would hope to hear "working for Pepsi, in the Toronto area, probably living in the downtown area and able to support my lifestyle." Nice.

The next logical question would be of course: "How are you going to accomplish this? What's the plan?" I refer to this piece in the previous chapter *Have You Started Your 2015 Personal Strategic Plan?*. But from the top…you can't have a plan without a vision.

A great leader needs to have a vision of the future. We can't just run forward into the market rudderless. We need direction. But the direction we are headed toward needs to be pointing to some end goal or a vision. We run our organizations with a strategic plan. But that plan is not possible if we don't know where we are going.

Once we have a vision of the future, clear and well-defined, we need to do two things:

- Create the plan.
- Communicate the vision to all involved.

One of the problems with organizations today is the lack of clarity – from the top to the bottom. A few key people may have created the vision, but was it well communicated to the team(s)?

That vision needs to be clearly communicated to the team(s) and there needs to be a sound plan in place to make it happen.

So what is your vision? For your department? For your company? For you? For your family? If you are struggling with this, then you are missing the key ingredient to success.

*Originally published April 23, 2014*

# SHOULD YOU IGNORE YOUR WEAKNESSES AND LEVERAGE YOUR STRENGTHS?

The *Globe and Mail*, one of our local newspapers here in Toronto, carried an article on August 27, 2014 by Harvey Schachter entitled "Ten Flawed Leadership Gems." He was quoting from a blog by Dan McCarthy out of the University of New Hampshire where Dan lists his take on 10 common leadership flaws.

One of them was "ignore your weaknesses and leverage your strengths." Remember, these are 10 *flawed* leadership traits.

Schachter wrote: "We're told we're paid for our strengths and need to develop them. But although research claims to show this is true, he notes that other research counters that advice – as does the logic of what we see around us in the workplace. 'The reality is that weaknesses matter. If the skill is important and you are weak, then you need to improve as it will hold you back,' [McCarthy] said. If your boss or a 360-degree evaluation identifies a weakness in an important area, be alert."

In the book I published with Derek Vigar, *The Keys to Our Success"*?, I contributed a chapter called "Never Go In Alone" where I suggest that we all need to find our weaknesses and fill the void. Take a course, hire a coach, consult with a mentor. There are many ways to fill the gap between your strengths and your weaknesses.

The hardest part, of course, is identifying the weakness and admitting to it. In my experience, it's not usually me who identifies the weakness but a boss, a peer, or – worse yet – a family member! And when we are first told that we are not a very good presenter, or we are a little short with some of the team or we need to work on our attention to detail, we do not take it well. My wife is my sounding board and my mirror. She is the one who will often tell me I need to fix some part of my professional life: an approach I take, a style of communication I use or a way I work with someone.

My current project? I get way too engaged, passionate and "over exuberant" for my own good. People don't like it. Or so I am told! Truthfully, I don't agree but this only goes to point out that this part of the exercise is the hardest.

I conducted a webinar today for the PMI IT & Telecom Community of Practice and found myself telling 800+ attendees that "the best of us, the strongest of us, will be able to look into a mirror, find the gaps and act on them." So should I. So should you.

Should we focus on our strengths? Of course. This is what makes us succeed. We leverage our strengths to be the best we can be in our field of endeavor. But do we ignore our weaknesses? Certainly not. This would be a huge mistake. Find them. Strategize a plan to fix them. Get some help and act.

Yes, I am working on my over exuberance. I am trying to tone it down!

I am told I have to work on my listening skills next. Ugh!

*Originally published September 10, 2014*

# PRESENTING

# MY TOP 3 TIPS FOR GREAT PRESENTATIONS

After the great response to my post "My 3 Tools to Conquer Your Fear of Presenting," I thought I would continue on the presentation line this week. "3 Tools" was about conquering your fear of presenting. Here we address my three tips for great presentations.

So what is a great presentation? How do we measure the success of a presentation? This is a pretty important question that needs to be addressed before you walk in front of an audience. As a keynote speaker, I measure my success by the number of people who come up to me afterward to talk to me and the immediate response from my primary sponsor. In a sales presentation, your success might be measured by a signature afterward, a commitment to another meeting or a favorable response from the customer. Whatever the position you are in, it is important to be sure you know why you are presenting, what you want out of it and how you will measure success.

When I talk about great presentations, it cannot be just about style and content, but rather did your presentation achieve the desired outcome.

My three tips today will apply to any presentation you embark on.

1. Passion

If your audience cannot feel your passion for the subject, your chances of success are less than otherwise. If you are passionate about the topic, the idea or the potential outcome, your audience will feel it and see it during your presentation. Passion is a key ingredient to the successful delivery of any message.

## 2. Uniqueness

Your presentations need to be memorable. If they are the "same old, same old," with basic visuals and typically common messages, success will be difficult to find. In my life, I have found that the more unique my presentations are, the better my chances are of success. I figure that uniqueness leads to memorable. And so often this is my objective.

To be unique, I use tools that most have not seen in a presentation. In a keynote scenario, I am always using Prezi (Prezi.com), an alternative to your basic PowerPoint. With large crowds, I use (www.polleverywhere.com) which allows me to poll the audience using their cell phones and text messaging. I try to embed videos in my presentations as often as I can, providing a break from the continuous output of words and text on the screen. I've even used videos completely unrelated to a presentation just to break the message in hopes that the total package becomes more memorable. I will always use a wireless mic and move around the audience.

In a selling situation, I might even leave the technology behind and create a very well-crafted whiteboard scene for the audience. This approach can stimulate better conversation after the presentation as everyone can see each section covered on the whiteboard.

Uniqueness is important in any selling or influencing role. Many people have come before you to communicate the same story or sell the same product. Your approach needs to be different and using unique tools and unique approaches can put your presentation a cut above the others.

## 3. Entertaining

The entertainment factor is often thought of as the domain of the keynote or inspirational speaker. As this is now a big part of my life, I'm constantly trying to find ways to entertain the audience as well as inspire and educate.

But the truth is that your presentation can be memorable not only through its uniqueness but its entertainment quality as well. I'm not suggesting a poorly placed joke but I am suggesting fun graphics, fun videos and even parts of the presentation that require some fun audience engagement. A good story is entertaining – one that ties the message to the audience. Sometimes, in a few circumstances, your visual appearance could be part of the entertainment – a well-placed hat, or sweater or a strategic pin. I have seen speakers get the audience physically involved or at least physically moving. Standing up to stretch, even 30 seconds of stretching to music. Getting people to move seats halfway through to encourage networking can be fun – very disruptive, but fun.

There are many ways to make your presentations more entertaining. You need to find that fun factor and get people smiling a little bit more. Entertainment leads to memorable.

So first be sure the desired outcome is very clear. Then think about the passion you are going to demonstrate, the uniqueness of your presentation and the fun factor. It all counts.

*Originally published January 28, 2015*

# 3 TOOLS TO CONQUER YOUR FEAR OF PRESENTING

The fear of presenting holds many people back in their careers.

It is said that less than 20% of the working population is comfortable presenting in public. That's a shame. So many positions that are waiting for us out there require great presentation skills.

This post is dedicated to anyone who needs to meet with a group of people and get a point across. This is not just for the professional speaker, the high-profile salesperson or the director of public relations. This is for all of us. Every leader needs to be able to present well. Every salesperson, regardless of their product or market, needs to be able to present well and that includes those selling over the phone. Managers at all levels need to be able to present well. Entrepreneurs, venture capitalists, great athletes and more all need to be great presenters.

The Fear of Presenting
We often think that improving our presentation skills is all about addressing our presence on stage or at the podium. This is really important. These are the basics, and are often the first things we learn about presenting: where to stand, where to look and how to project. But when it comes to presenting well, we need to address the elephant in the room: our fear. The most important element to good public speaking is conquering our fears. If you have less trepidation and more confidence, the basics will come more naturally.

Here are my three tools that, used properly, will help to conquer your fear of presenting and thus become a better, if not a great, speaker.

## 1. Know Your Audience

Before you present to any group, you need to sit in their seats and understand why they are there. You need to ask yourself what they are looking for from you. Why are they here? What is the best outcome for them at the end of the session? What questions or objections might they have after this presentation?

Preempting your audience's reaction is so important when presenting. With all of this information, if it's available to you, you can frame your message so that it comes out right the first time. Ideally you are going to cover all of their needs. Truthfully you may not know exactly what they are thinking nor how they will react – but that's alright. Knowing these gaps is just as important.

Watching someone in front of me present an idea and correctly anticipate issues or questions I might have is a very pleasant surprise. Your audience wants you to know that you know them. And most important, your knowledge of their position, situation or needs will help in the battle of your nerves.

## 2. Have a Plan

You need to have a set plan before you step in front of the audience. What are your objectives? What do you want to get out of the session? How will you address your audience's needs, problems or issues? What is the key message and how are you going to frame it? And while you are at it, why not ask yourself how you can make this a memorable moment in your audience's life. These ideas sound lofty and ideal, but if you don't address them beforehand and embed them in a plan, you are risking the desired outcome. One more tool that, if applied properly, will contribute a little more to the battle of the nerves.

## 3. Clarity

There is nothing worse than sitting in a presentation that is scattered, disorganized and all over the map. You need to be very clear with your audience about the message, the process and the objectives. Tell them right up front what you are about to tell them. Tell them how long you are going to be with them and how you are going to present to them.

Show them the big picture at the front end and then start drilling down into each section. At the end, come back to the big picture and tell them what you wanted to tell them, where you've been and where you stand now. Guide them carefully and logically through your journey. Structure and clarity is the third key to battling your nerves.

Conquer your presentation nerves and you will discover the power of presenting well. Leave the nerves (or most of them) behind and you can start to concentrate on the basics and more.

Understand your audience, have a plan and be very clear in your message.

*Originally published December 12, 2014*

# PROJECT MANAGEMENT

# CAN PROJECT MANAGERS BECOME SENIOR CORPORATE LEADERS?

Project managers are the best-equipped employees to take on roles as senior leaders. They just need a little training.

A great leader would:

- be a great people person – be compassionate.
- be a visionary – can see the big picture and communicate the plan.
- have a strong business acumen – can talk to authority, stakeholders and shareholders.
- be a great quarterback – can guide us to the win, execute the plan.
- have a process-driven approach to work – have a system that is reliable and repeatable.

The great news for the project management community is that they have three of the five qualities – and these are the attributes most difficult to find!

So what? Project managers need to look outside the comfort of their "on time, on budget, on scope" world and reach for the senior leadership positions within their organizations. They are prime candidates.

A great project manager should already be very good with people (#1). If not, they won't be around long. The quarterback thing (#4) is a little more difficult to quantify but the great project managers I know are great quarterbacks: structured, visible, easy to get along with and very easy to follow.

A process-driven approach (#5) should be a slam dunk for any good project manager. They cannot manage a project without a process. A really good project manager will come to the table with process as part of his/her core competency. They know how to execute a plan – how to get the work done.

How can they fill the gaps?

To become a great leader, they need to understand the business. They need to be able to work at a level far above the detail, to be able to see the vision (even to be able to create the vision) and manage the business.

I would love to say "quit your job and take an MBA" but I can't – risky, inaccessible for many, overkill for most. Instead, here are my tips for closing the skills gap – evolving from a good project manager to a great leader.

1. *Understand how to manage change.*
Change is a reality in every business environment. Economies change, people change and customers come and go. Change is a part of every leader's daily life and he/she had better understand how to embrace it. This is not part of every PM's fabric so there is a gap here.

2. *Learn a new language.*
My friend Gary Heerkens calls this the CxO language (CEO, CFO, CIO, etc.). Understanding how to talk to power is critical – so learn how to talk their language. If you want, get involved in the business at a level above the project management circles. You need to understand how to read a balance sheet and income statement. You need to understand how to calculate ROI and NPV. And you need to be able to make a cash flow statement sing.

3. *Connect your work to the business.*
A very smart friend of mine, Ken Robertson, tells the aspiring PM to understand "business outcome." By this he means connect to the real purpose of your work. Where does it fit into the big picture? How does it

connect to the strategic plan? Start worrying about the portfolio of projects rather than just the projects.

4. *Get out of your comfort zone – manage projects in other areas.*
If you stay in IT forever, you will never be a valuable leader to the organization. Get out of where you are and into something different. Ask for a position in a completely different area. Expand your knowledge and experience. Tomorrow's most valuable leaders know the business – all of it.

Project managers, the really good ones, should feel very excited about their future. They have the core to great leadership – which most others do not. Filling the gaps should be easy.

Can project managers become senior corporate leaders? Absolutely.

*Originally published January 27, 2014*

# WHAT DOES A PROJECT MANAGEMENT OFFICE LOOK LIKE?

Someone recently asked me about a one-day seminar on building a project management office (PMO). I told them that there could be no greater waste of time than to get an individual to stand in front of them for one day to tell them how to build the PMO. And if they did, I guarantee that that office would be closed within a few years.

When talking about the PMO, I love to say that, at last count, there are 2,456 variations on the theme. My point is that no project office will be the same in any organization and nor should it. And no individual or training organization has the answer.

About 10 to 12 years ago, the PMO became the fad across many industries but especially within IT, and many organizations launched their first project management office. I was running ProjectWorld Canada at the time and we ran many sessions, hearing from organizations about how they developed their PMO. It was all good news. But then a funny thing happened: four to five years later, those same organizations were quietly admitting that those original PMOs had closed.

Why? Because they were built for the wrong reasons, for the wrong people and by the wrong people.

I talk about leadership most of the time. Is this discussion about leadership? I certainly think it is. You see, leadership does not have to come from just people but it can come from processes or organizations that we create. In this case, the PMO is a perfect leadership tool. In my mind, its role is to lead the project management community in any way that it is asked to do. These last words are the key to the successful PMO:

*that it is asked to do.*

I've seen the virtual PMO whose job it is to set standards, create guidelines and advise when necessary. This version is run by contributions from multiple parts of a department or organization.

I've seen the PMO that directly employs 20 to 30 people with a director-level lead, a budget and a performance requirement. This group is typically opening and closing large projects and often directly managing the largest, most mission-critical projects. Much more hands-on and a lot more responsibility.

And in the middle, as I have said, there are 2,000+ variations of these models.

So what's the right answer? I don't have it and no one should profess to have the answer for you either. The key to success lies in the same method you would use to create a new custom software program or build a new product: you need to ask the customer.

If you know me, you might know that I have been very involved in the creation and the development of the International Institute for Business Analysis. Now, don't leave me. This is not a pitch for the IIBA. But it is a pitch for the role of the business analyst. Whether professionally trained and certified or "winging it," someone needs to play the role of the business analyst.

Before anyone talks about the virtual PMO, hiring employees or creating roles and responsibilities, we need to step back and do a full needs analysis with the customer and all stakeholders. We need to model any potential solutions back to the customer to be sure we are heading in the right direction. We need to make everyone aware of the costs, risks and rewards of a potential solution to their needs. In the end, we need to make sure that every stakeholder is aware of what is to be built and what is involved in doing so. And we need to get everyone's buy-in not only in supporting the build but supporting the new product going into the future.

If you ever wondered what the business analyst does, this is the perfect description. I like to tell BAs and project management communities that the role of the BA is to be sure that when it is built, it is built right the first time. I like to say that the BA's role is to make sure that there aren't eight revisions because the audience wasn't properly involved.

What does a project management office look like? I can show you examples and models. But – like the final look of your new kitchen – I can't give you the answer quite yet. I need time to figure out what you really want, what you can afford and what you can support. Then I can tell you what your project management office might look like.

*Originally published March 18, 2015*

# WHAT IS A SPONSOR CHARTER?

The relationship between the project sponsor and the project manager or project leader is extremely important and yet we spend so little time making sure we get it right.

We have all heard of the project charter. We take the necessary time up front to be sure we are all paddling in the same direction. And some of us have heard of the team charter. For those of us that use this important tool, we always see the benefits of understanding the team before we head out into battle.

But a sponsor charter?

Why not? If the project leader's relationship with the sponsor is so important, why not create a new tool called the sponsor charter to help the two roles really understand each other.

Before I present the outline of this new tool, I must admit that I think I know why the concept of a sponsor charter doesn't exist already. The difference in positions between the (typically) executive sponsor and the project manager is often so great that this kind of care for the "relationship" is unheard of. So, the key to success here is that this new tool needs to be mandated from the senior level. In fact, let's get the sponsor's buy-in first and then hand it to the project managers to implement.

So here is the new sponsor charter.

Part 1 – Know the Person

Establish a common thread outside of the work at hand.

I know this is going to sound a little fluffy to some of you but this first step is really important for any new professional connection. This is where you get to know the "person" across from you.

The sponsor/project leader relationship is typically a brand-new connection for you both and you are going to be working together for a long time. If you take the time to find a common thread between the two of you from outside the business at hand, you will find the work and the relationship more enjoyable and more rewarding – for both of you. Regardless of how senior your sponsor is, they have a life outside of work. Look around the office. Look at photos of family and vacations, notice the plaques on the wall and look at the books on the shelf. Somewhere out there, there is a common thread between you. A shared love of basketball, kids the same age or a favorite author. Find it. Pull it out for a few minutes and establish a lighter side to this new relationship. It is important to make this initial personal connection to your sponsor. It can pay off in many ways.

Part 2 – Know Your Sponsor

The next step is to get to know the "sponsor" across the table as opposed to the "person." This is the 'intelligence' that you need to make this partnership work well. A lot of key questions come to mind but I want to highlight the most important one: "Have you ever been a project sponsor before?" This does not necessarily have to be a question but rather just some good old research before the first meeting. If the answer is no, you will need to approach the front end of this project a little differently than otherwise. The kiss of death for any of us is a project sponsor who hasn't got a clue as to what they are doing. If you are in this position, then you need to know fast. Ideally this knowledge will lead to an enthusiasm for learning more about the role – from you of course. So be prepared.

Other questions you need answers to fairly quickly:

- If they have been a sponsor before, how did it go? What worked? What didn't?
- If not, would they be open to suggestions, guidance or even training? (I know of a large corporation that puts all project sponsors through a half-day training program.)
- How do they manage their workday?
- How do they like to communicate (email format, report length, etc.)?
- What bugs them when dealing with project people?
- What do they like about project people?
- What other projects are they sponsoring that might affect their response to you and your project?

Part 3 – Make Sure Your Sponsor Knows You

As important as you knowing all about them, it is as important that they know all about you.


- Your strengths
- Your weaknesses
- How you manage your time
- The best way to find you and/or communicate with you


And what other project(s) are you working on that might affect your response to him/her and this project?

Part 4 – Establish the Rules of Engagement

Finally, how are you going to work together? Where will you meet, for how long and what will your meetings look like? How involved will each of you get in critical areas of the project, including conflict and budget issues and more? How much does he/she want to know about the minutia of the project? What do you do when (not if) certain parts of the plan fall off the rails?

The sponsor charter helps to establish a relationship and rules of engagement for both parties. As with the team charter and the project chapter, this is a crucial tool of today's project leaders. Would this work in your organization?

*Originally published December 3, 2014*

# ARE YOU PROJECT MANAGING MORE THAN YOU ARE MANAGING YOUR PROJECT?

One of the most common mistakes a new project manager makes is that they spend more time project managing than they do managing their projects.

Whether we are newcomers to the project management business or experienced pros, we need to remind ourselves that our project success can be seriously threatened by our rigid approach to the use of tools, processes and procedures.

Have you ever caught yourself spending way too much time on the best-looking Gantt chart at the expense of more time spent on more worthy project start-up work? Have you ever found yourself pumping out required reports that no one will read?

Project management at the expense of managing projects.

Paul Bergman wrote in his chapter "Scalability and Common Sense" in the book *The Keys to Our Success* that successful project managers need to be able to scale their use of common tools to fit the proper environment. He is primarily referring to technical tools like scheduling software, but I would extend his thought process to presentations, meetings and other nontechnical "tools" that we have available to us. The key to success, he writes, is understanding when to use each tool and even if you should use it at all. It is understanding how much of a tool you apply in each scenario and, as important, whether you have the right tools or not.

We "over–project manage" when we:

- spend too much time creating the schedule and not enough time doing the work.
- build a schedule to a detail far too great for the project at hand.
- worry too much about following a standard methodology or process.
- think too hard about, and spend too much time dealing with, project risks that have far too small a chance of occurring.
- conduct too many meetings that are not relevant to all of the attendees.

We should be more concerned about managing the project as we:

- focus on our clients, our team and our sponsors.
- create an environment of clear, simple and precise communication within all stakeholders of the project.
- scale down the use of our standard tools to fit each different project.
- get our heads into the business case behind the project.

As you head into your next project, put yourself in the seat of your customer, your team and your sponsors and ask yourself what they need to be successful. Then pick up the right tool, use the right strength and set the right level of communication across all stakeholders and make it happen.

*Originally published February 11, 2015*

# DO YOU KICK OFF YOUR PROJECTS WITH A TEAM CHARTER

I do a lot of public speaking these days and one of my presentations deals briefly with the team charter. I always take the opportunity to ask the audience how many people actually create a team charter at the front end of a project. The response has never been more than a sprinkling of hands in the audience. I find this staggering.

An executive at EDS said to me years ago: "Managing projects could be much easier if it weren't for the people. It's the people that make project management so difficult." This is absolutely true. But isn't it funny that we don't spend the time at the front dealing with this crucial piece of the puzzle? Most of us can say that we create great project charters but I think most projects are missing this vitally important tool.

Why aren't people creating a team charter? I think there are a number of reasons for this. Unfortunately, people don't get that the people side of our projects is so important. I think others have no idea how to create one so they ignore it. And I think many others think it takes way too much time, effort and even money so they plow on into the project without any consideration of the team.

The truth is that the team charter can be created easily, quickly and for absolutely no money at all if done properly. If I were to be asked to manage a large five-year, $50-million initiative, I would certainly invest a little money and get my team out of the office for at least a day to create the team charter. If I were to be asked to manage a small but important project, I might just take one or two hours at the front end.

So what does the team charter look like? The team charter should deal with two very different things: the team as a group and each individual.

The team issues we want to deal with include (but are not limited to):

- Who is on the team?
- How will we work together as a team?
- How will we communicate?
- Do we want to set up some rules of engagement?

Note that some of this sounds like outputs from our communications plan. What? You don't do that either?

Turning to individual team members:

- What are your strengths?
- What are your weaknesses?
- Do you have special skills or talents that might help us?
- What kinds of personalities are we dealing with?
- Are there any constraints we should know about regarding your involvement in this project?

A friend of mine, Catherine Daw, former president of SPM Group, contributed a chapter to the book *The Keys to Our Success – Lessons Learned from 25 of Our Best Project Managers* that dealt with leadership style. Daw suggests that we should understand our own leadership styles and learn where to apply the different styles within different occasions. When I talk about this chapter in some of my speeches, I highlight the need for not only understanding your own leadership style but the importance of communicating this to your team. They need to understand your leadership style as much as you need to know your own. I mention this because the team charter isn't just about the team. It is as much about the leadership of the team as well. And that is you. After you ask your team members to reveal their strengths and weaknesses, you had better be able to do so as well.

The list above includes "What kinds of personalities are we dealing with?" Examining our personality styles as part of a team charter can provide a very valuable view of your team members. This is not just for you, the project manager, of course, but for everyone's benefit. If I know that someone is a "hawk" and not a "dove" or a "red" and not a "green," it will help me with my dealings with everyone on the team.

I have always thought that this was a very expensive and time-consuming tool so I have never considered its use at the front end of a project. Until recently. I watched a keynote speaker take a crowd of 200 through 20 questions, self-scoring as they went along, in under 10 minutes. She then had everyone total their scores and move to a corner of the room with the personalities most like their own. Brilliant. The tool was simple, quick and *free*! Great for a conference and maybe that small project. But for the "all-important, make-or-break-us" project, spend some money and do it right. There are very good personality assessment tools out there.

The team charter helps to pull together your troops, create a healthy work environment and – very important – it builds a strong foundation for the people side of your project.

Will you take the time on your next project to create a team charter?

*Originally published May 28, 2014*

# CLOSE TO HOME

# FOUR THINGS MY WIFE LEARNED ABOUT LEADERSHIP WHILE VOLUNTEERING AT THE PAN AM GAMES

In case you didn't know it, the Pan Am Games are in full swing now in Toronto. I know this very well because my wife, Karen, is a volunteer at the Games. As I've watched her come and go from her commitments these past two weeks, I've learned a lot, not only about her, but as well about the lessons that volunteering can provide to leaders.

It is often said that great leaders not only lead but they serve as well. The service leadership concept is based on the philosophy of servant leadership, a term coined by Robert K. Greenleaf to define a leader who is a servant first.

From the book *Public and Third Sector Leadership: Experience Speaks* by Brian Howieson and Julie Hodges "The servant-leader shares power, puts the needs of others first and helps people develop and perform as highly as possible."

Those who volunteer and serve in any capacity understand that the experience contributes to their lives (and of course many others) at so many levels.

This has been a real eye-opener for Karen but I look at what she comes home with and think about how this experience (or any like it) can help all leaders.

Leadership lessons Karen has learned from volunteering at the Toronto 2015 Pan Am Games

1. *Managing people at any level is extremely difficult.* Karen is about three levels from the one person who manages her whole site. She has one direct manager and three people below her who in turn manage about 15 people each. It's huge. This facility alone has 600 volunteers. In just the first two weeks of her four-week commitment, she has seen it all: from bright and energetic people day in and day out to others who don't even show up for a day or two. Complainers to problem solvers. The process and structure are easy. It's the people that make it so difficult. Sixty thousand people applied to volunteer at these Games for only 23,000 positions. Yes, Toronto is a large metropolis but that's a lot of people willing to give their time and effort to a cause. But are they going to get it right every time? No way. Is everyone on the team there for the right reasons? Are they all willing to pull their weight for the cause? At an event like this, or our own organizations, it's the people who will provide us with the biggest challenges.

2. *Watching and learning is the best line to gaining experience.* Leadership requires a very fine touch when it comes to dealing with the team, and Karen has been able to see great leadership and terrible leadership in action. You see it firsthand, think about how you would have approached it and store the learning in the vault.

3. *Agility is a critical skill for leaders.* I am amazed to hear that – with all the layers of management these folks have set up – they are able to adjust the plan on the fly. Each day, it seems, they are looking at what went right and what went wrong, changing the plan and communicating it to the next team coming in for the next shift.

4. *Saying thank-you goes a long way.* OK, get this: every volunteer gets a small gift of thanks at the end of each shift. A pin, funky plastic sunglasses, a trinket of some kind. Small, inexpensive – but incredibly powerful. And all the managers at Karen's level and higher have been trained to visit each and every team member to check in, say thanks and be sure they are alright. Leaders at all levels need to learn from this. Get down into the trenches and show our appreciation. Karen reminds me that this simple act makes everyone feel so important.

Karen is exhausted after some very long 12-hour shifts. But this has been an amazing experience for her. She has met some very nice people all with the common idea that serving is important. She is not moving into or going back to a senior leadership position after these Games but her take-aways are just as important as those who are in a ship position.

For those leaders and future leaders working the Games, I think they will go away with some great takeaways about great leadership.

And for all the rest of us, where are we serving? Where are we experiencing the thrill of giving back and the upside of learning about leadership firsthand?

*Originally published July 22, 2015*

# THINGS I LEARNED AT OUR SPECIAL CANADIAN THANKSGIVING WEEKEND

This past weekend was Canadian Thanksgiving. In our family this is always a very busy weekend with 20 to 30 of us gathering in the Collingwood area north of Toronto for a big dinner. But this year was very different.

I come from a family of five. The youngest is our sister, who now lives far away and she was married this weekend – in Collingwood. So our traditional, slightly large Thanksgiving dinner celebration became a very large four-day affair including a wedding, a separate Thanksgiving dinner under a rented tent, flying tours over the area, a tennis tournament, a bike trip and more for upwards of 50 people.

Today we wake up with mixed emotions: it was an amazing weekend that we will never forget and we are really glad it's over. This weekend was a lot of work for a lot of people. But there were some lessons learned that I thought I would share with you.

1. From my wife: it takes a village. The weekend involved months of preparation. The actual three to four days involved coordination, hard work and certainly some stress for some. But in the end, our success came as a result of the many people helping out in so many different parts of the puzzle. In each separate part, we watched someone stand up and take ownership. During the execution of each part, we witnessed many more people rally around to help out. It does take a village to execute events like this. Leadership is important but without the rest of the village enthusiastically following and executing, this kind of event will never be successful.

We certainly learned that there doesn't have to be any glory in that leadership role. As a strong leader at any level, we should be able to enjoy the simple fact that it went off without a hitch and that everyone had a fabulous time. There is no need for an award ceremony or a letter of thanks to one person. The village knows it did well and we all take pride in the results.

2. From one of my brothers: people can be so appreciative of the smallest thing. I love this. We do tend to think about the big splash and the big event and the big applause. But the smallest thing can certainly make a difference. My sister was thrilled with the set-up for Thanksgiving dinner: the tent set up in the yard, the tables set for 40+ people, the beautiful candles and more. But the truth is that what she loved the most were the little details that we included from all the traditional Thanksgiving dinners that she missed during her years in Denver. Our song that we use for grace. The silly little wooden houses that we build as place cards for all of our guests during these special dinners.

In life and at work, many of us perform small tasks, play minor roles within an organization, contribute small parts to larger projects and forget how important these small things can be. There are very few accolades, and often no thanks, but we do make a difference. And just when you think that no one has noticed, someone will come along one day to offer a heartfelt thank-you. This makes all of our work so worthwhile.

3. From my daughter: don't present the problem, just tell me the solution. This goes back to a decision that had to be made about some part of the weekend. I saw a problem and proceeded to tell the problem to as many family members who would listen. And my daughter turns around with this line. She certainly caught me by surprise. She was quite right. I was wasting everyone's time. What she wanted was a solution to the problem. This way she and others could look at a proposed changeup and weigh in on the potential results.

Maybe we do waste too much time preaching the problem. I will try to preach the solution next time.

4. My last lesson learned is a reminder of how important one special role is in any event like ours when timing is tight, there are a lot of moving parts and it involves a lot of people: the gofer.

One of my children decided that she would stand in the middle of all the Thanksgiving preparation chaos and be on call to anyone who needed help. There were five "prime cooks" in the kitchen, three others carving the turkeys, four others setting up for the food presentation, five others setting the tables and more. She stood up at the beginning and declared herself as the go-to person for anyone who needed any help at all. Brilliant.

I thought afterward of the many conferences I have run over the past 17 years, of the numerous charity events I have been involved with and the many large family dinners I have helped with and I realize how important this role is.

It was a lovely wedding that my family will never forget. It was a great Thanksgiving dinner. The flying tours were amazing, the tennis was fun and the traditional family walk on Sunday was wonderful as usual.

But I learned a few things along the way. I think others did as well.

*Originally published October 14, 2014*

# ABOUT THE AUTHOR

David is the National Program Director for Project Management and Business Analysis with the Schulich Executive Education Centre, Schulich School of Business, York University, Toronto.

He is also a regular blogger, podcaster and professional speaker specializing in leadership, strategy execution and professional growth.

He has published three books: The Power of The Plan, The Keys to Our Success and the Business Analyst Book of Mentors.

Previously, he was the Group Conference Director at Diversified Business Communications where he ran project management and business analysis events around the world and he was the Executive Editor and founder of ProjectTimes.com and BATimes.com.

He is the father of 4 and the grandfather of 2 (at time of writing) of 2. He lives in Port Credit, Ontario.

# OTHER BOOKS FROM DAVID BARRETT

**The Keys to Our Success – Lessons Learned from 25 of Our Best Project Managers.**

Published in 2013 by David Barrett and Derek Vigar

What we continually see from conferences, industry events, and post-secondary classrooms is keen interest from those in the project management profession to connect with and learn from the best. So, we approached those widely regarded as industry leaders and asked them a straightforward question: "What is the best piece of advice you would share for success in project management?

The result is this book—a collection of their best stories, lessons, and takeaways. 25 different industry leaders make 25 different compelling cases for why their "key" will help influence your project success:

• The seven bullets of highly effective project managers
• Why leadership must be taken, not given
• The importance of becoming project "business-savvy"
• Ways to generate meaningful client ownership
• How great project managers make it fun
• And 20 other differentiators that have helped these industry leaders stand out.

If you're interested in what's really important to differentiate yourself and take the next step in your project management career, then this book is a fantastic opportunity to connect with trusted mentors, read honest advice from people who have been there, and start to incorporate these keys to success into your own practice.

Available from Amazon.com or direct from the publisher: www.mmpubs.com

## The Business Analysis Book of Mentors – 25 Lessons Learned from Seasoned BA Professionals

Published in 2014 by David Barrett and Sandee Vincent

The most accomplished people attribute their success, to a large part, to their mentors.

Bill Gates had Warren Buffett, Mark Zuckerberg had Steve Jobs, Wayne Gretzky had Garnet Bailey, Oliver Stone had Martin Scorsese, and even Luke Skywalker had a mentor in Obi-wan Kenobi.

Mentors provide insight and guidance in challenging situations and help you avoid the pitfalls. And in business analysis, there are many pitfalls to navigate around.

Now you have your own 25 mentors, well-seasoned in business analysis, inside this book. Your mentors provide advice such as how not to look stupid, what kind of questions to ask, how to grasp the big picture quickly, how to respond when told to 'just get on with it already', and when you should just keep your mouth shut.
If you are interested in some advice from some of the best business analysts out there, then this book is a great opportunity to connect with them.

Available from Amazon.com or direct from the publisher:
www.mmpubs.com

## The Power of the Plan – 10 Easy Steps to Managing Everyday Projects

Published in 2013 by David Barrett and Douglas Land

How many of us have offered to run a small project in our lives only to discover mid-way through that we really did not have a good grasp of the art of managing a project?

How many of us would like to step-up and volunteer our time to run a project but feel we do not have the necessary tools.

This book presents a simple, easy-to-understand process for managing small, everyday projects. This is not "Project Management Essentials" or "PM 101". It is simpler than that.

We will take you through a series of 10 steps for managing a small everyday project starting with the important question "Should I really do this?" all the way through to tips on closing it all down and celebrating at the end. We will show you how to run great meetings that people want to attend, how to create a simple schedule, budget and more. Most importantly, we will give you the tools to deliver your project on time and on budget making you and others feel great about your results.

This book is here to empower you to say "Yes, I can run that event" and to give the tools to make it happen.

Available from Amazon.com or direct from the publisher: www.mmpubs.com